# Animals with Fins, Animals with Fur

written by Kelly Gaffney

Dear Uncle Jarrad,

How are you?
I'm well, but I have been very busy at school.
This week, I did my first *school project*.
It was about animals with fins and animals with fur.
I want to tell you some of the things
that I found out.

There are animals that have fins.
Fins help them to swim in the water.
*Dolphins* have fins and so do *whales*.
Fish have fins and so do *sharks*.

2

Sharks are fish, but whales and dolphins are not.

Some fins are little and some fins are big.
Little fish have small fins,
but a whale has fins that are enormous.

This fish has little fins.

This whale has a very big fin.

This little fish needs to swim very fast!

Fins help the animal to swim fast or slow.
They help it to swim towards its food,
or away from something that is chasing it.
Fins can make the animal turn.
They also stop it from rolling over in the water.
I wish I had fins, so I could swim faster!

I also found out about animals with fur.
Fur is the thick *hair* that some animals
have on their skin.
It helps the animal to keep warm
when the *weather* is cool.
Fur can be long or short.

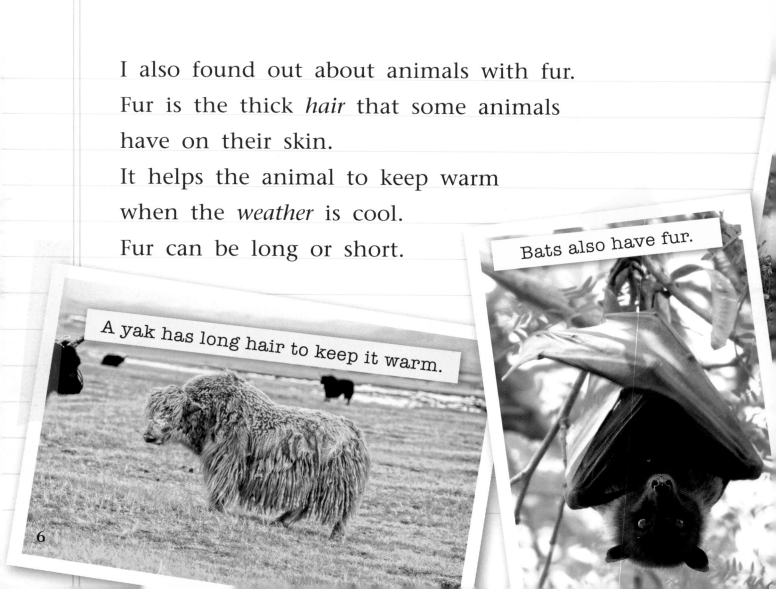

A yak has long hair to keep it warm.

Bats also have fur.

*Yaks* have long fur but bats have short fur.
Dogs, cats and *monkeys* can have long or short fur.

A rabbit has fur that is very soft.
This makes them good to hold.

This rabbit has soft fur.

A hedgehog's *spines* are made of hair.

*Hedgehogs* have fur but they are **not** good to hold!

Most animals with fur live on the land,
but some of them spend a lot of time in the water.
When *fur seals* and *otters* are in the water,
their thick fur keeps them warm.

This fur seal is swimming in the water.

This otter is swimming in the water, too.

The colour of an animal's fur can help it to hide.
A *lion's* fur helps it to hide in the long grass.
A *polar bear's* white fur makes it hard to see
on the ice.

Some *foxes* have white fur in *winter*
and brown fur in *summer* to help them hide.

That is everything I have found out
about animals with fins and animals with fur.

Next week we will be finding out about *volcanoes*.
I will tell you all about volcanoes, too!

Love,
Nick

Animals with Fins

Animals with Fur

# Picture glossary

dolphins

lion

sharks

whales

foxes

otters

spines

winter

fur seals

monkeys

summer

yaks

hair

polar bear

volcanoes

hedgehogs

school project

weather